Dreams You Can Count On
Visual Art and Mathematics

Twelve Standards-Based Lessons for
Classroom and Art Teachers K-6

14th Edition

BINNEY &SMITH® A Hallmark Company

Easton, Pennsylvania

Credits

© 2004, Binney & Smith, Inc., Easton, Pennsylvania USA

Director of Education

Richard Stringer

For Crayola® Dream-Makers® 14, *Dreams You Can Count On*:
Author and Managing Editor

Ron DeLong

Editors

Janet Brown McCracken
Donna Chastain

Photographer

Peter M. Sak

Editorial Assistance by

Diana K. Sparrow

For Crayola.com Dream-Makers Resources:

Jacqualyne M. Flynn

Kutztown University Student Teachers:

Kate Dussinger
Trista Herrlin
Rami Steinruck

Binney & Smith gratefully acknowledges the teachers who tested the lessons in this guide:

Barbi Bailey-Smith, Carly Doughty, and Janice House, Little River Elementary School, Durham, North Carolina
Pat Check, Spring Garden Elementary School, Bethlehem, Pennsylvania
Neila Steiner, C.S. 102, Bronx, New York
Kay LaBella and Karen Sommerfeld, Foothills Elementary School, Colorado Springs, Colorado
Lynn Schatzle, Wood Creek Elementary School, Farmington Hills, Michigan
Nancy Rhoads, Curlew Creek Elementary School, Palm Harbor, Florida
Jen O'Flaherty and Rob Bartoch, Sandy Plains Elementary School, Baltimore, Maryland
Barbara Grasso, John J. Jennings Elementary School, Bristol, Connecticut
Elyse Martin and Trish Davlantes, Michael Jordan Community School, Chicago, Illinois
Charlotte Ka, PS 132K, Brooklyn, New York
Jennifer Parks, T. J. Lee Elementary School, Irving, Texas

Additional thanks for their assistance and support to:

Gary Fassak
Cheri Sterman
Barbara Benton
Elizabeth H. Willett
Jill C. Jamison
Charles Mc Anall

Front cover: Photograph by Peter M. Sak, Art Direction by Ron DeLong, Student artwork by students from John J. Jennings Elementary School, Bristol, CT. Teacher: Barbara Grasso

Design

First Generation Productions, Allentown, Pennsylvania

Karen Spinney, Designer

Alexandra Shade, Producer

Crayola, Dream-Makers, chevron, serpentine, Overwriters, Artista II, Classpack and Model Magic are registered trademarks; Smile design, Construction Paper, Premier, and Rocket Minds are trademarks of Binney & Smith.

Printed in the United States of America

ISBN: 0-86696-316-2

Table of Contents

Introduction   4

Alliances, Collaborations and Exhibitions   5

About Crayola® Dream-Makers®   6

How to Use Dream-Makers   7

National Visual Arts Standards   8

Standards for School Mathematics   9

Lessons for Grades K-2

Counting on a Spectacular Garden   10

In the Face of Symmetry   12

Gee's-ometric Wisdom   14

Patterns of Love Beads   16

Lessons for Grades 3-4

A Bountiful Table—Sharing Fairly   18

Whimsical Charting and Checking   20

Counting Shapes Among the Splatter   22

Toying Around With Geometry   24

Lessons for Grades 5-6

Measure Twice, Create Once   26

The Average Time—You See   28

Purchasing Flower Power   30

Personal Illusions—Raising Your Banner High   32

Art Images   34

Introduction

While exploring the relationship between visual arts and math for this new edition of the Crayola® Dream-Makers® guide, I had to confront a negative math memory from my early schooling. When I came up with a correct answer more quickly than other children in the class, my teacher suspected that I had cheated.

I solved the problem, but not the way the teacher expected me to solve it. "Do it the right way!" I was told. This experience triggers anxieties to this day—for years, I considered myself "math-challenged." Not long ago, in order to address my perceived deficiency, I arranged a professional math assessment. The results showed that I measure up. Could it be that this early trauma inhibited my mastery of a crucial skill? This led me to ask the question, "How should we teach math?" The stage was set for a challenge!

My solution was to strengthen my personal understanding of how closely interrelated visual arts and math can be, and should be, for children's educational success. Looking back, I recall dreaming of being successful in both subjects. I was pleased to discover that researchers tell us that if we combine logical math principles with visual arts, previously unclear concepts can come into focus and understanding will suddenly click for the students.

Mathematicians and scientists, Einstein included, have said that they rely more on mental signs and images than words in doing their work. This is borne out by brain-imaging research showing that approximate calculations take place in the brain's large-scale network, which also does visual, spatial and analogical mental transformations. In contrast, rote arithmetic takes place in areas usually reserved for verbal tasks. This exploration of higher-order brain functions has far-reaching implications for math education.

One of my dreams has been to create a practical, visually engaging art and math resource that will enhance both academic disciplines. Mathematics has deep roots in art history (see page 6). For children who learn more readily through visual or tactile lessons, consider their delight in unraveling the mysteries of number concepts through art history, in exploring fractions and averages through their knowledge of structures and functions. This approach can truly bring all learners forward—leaving none behind!

We must help children dream. We must cultivate their desires to become spectacular artists. We must construct strategies that grow exceptional mathematicians. We must invent opportunities that inspire emerging engineers and scientists, but most important, we must enrich children's abilities to find multiple solutions to life's challenges.

Crayola Dream-Makers *Dreams You Can Count On—Visual Art and Mathematics* is a resource that encourages and inspires success in two discrete disciplines through 12 standards-based lessons. We focused the content to help students who may have difficulty with conventional math rules, allowing them to "see" how math makes sense, by combining logical math concepts with hands-on activities. As we consider how best to teach math to all students today, we hope that you will consider this guide as a resource for your program. Collaborate with your peers to invigorate children's capacity to learn. Together, our efforts will benefit children as they grow, find success, and come to understand that it is their DREAMS THAT COUNT.

— Ron DeLong

Below: *Hommage to Einstein*, by Antonio Garcia, watercolor on paper. 22" x 30", Corpus Christie, TX, 1975. Collection of Eduardo and Antonina Garcia

Alliances and Collaborations

Educational Alliances

Since 1984, the Crayola Dream-Makers program has involved millions of students and thousands of teachers in art-related educational activities. Along with our partners—the National Art Education Association and the John F. Kennedy Center for the Performing Arts—we believe the arts are fundamental to the creative development of all children. Through the efforts of these key partners, the Crayola Dream-Makers program helps strengthen art education in the classroom and community, provides hands-on resources and participation opportunities for students and their teachers, and recognizes students for their creative efforts.

National Art Education Association

Founded in 1947, the National Art Education Association is the largest professional art education association in the world. Membership includes teachers, administrators, museum educators, arts council staff and university professors from the United States and 66 foreign countries. NAEA's mission is to advance art education through professional development, service, research, and leadership. For more information about the NAEA, call (703) 860-8000.

The John F. Kennedy Center for the Performing Arts

Since 1974, the Kennedy Center's IMAGINATION CELEBRATION National Sites program has sponsored year-round programs in the arts, for young people and their families. IMAGINATION CELEBRATION sites in Dallas, Fort Worth, Seattle, Colorado Springs, Orange County, CA, and Salt Lake City reflect community-wide partnerships between cultural resources and schools, businesses, professional and civic organizations and local governments. In addition, Kennedy Center Partners-in-Education sites in Williamsport, PA, Madisonville, KY, and Hilton Head, SC foster partnerships between arts organizations and local school systems, with a special emphasis on professional development of teachers. For more information about the Kennedy Center's programs, call (202) 416-8000.

Collaboration Works!

Understanding that collaboration is a key to success in schools, we developed the lessons in this guide to encourage and support collaborative work. Although individual teachers can easily present lessons, we have broken out preparation steps and discussion starters to simplify teamwork and/or peer consultation. Of course, teachers benefit when tasks are shared, but students also benefit when they see more than one adult supporting their efforts.

Besides fellow art or classroom teachers, any of the following could have a place on your team:

New teachers	Reading specialists
Librarians	Parents
Artists from your community	Art groups or local art agencies

Here are some steps for a successful team process. This can work whether you are jointly presenting a lesson over a few class periods, or putting on a school or community-wide exhibition.

1. First, share this guide with your collaborators before your first meeting, so they have an idea of what to expect.

2. Meet to agree on your goals and develop an action plan. Identify the steps you need to take, and decide who will be responsible for each.

3. Make a calendar that includes the important milestones and allows adequate time for each process.

4. Work your plan. Have periodic meetings or phone calls to make sure you keep on track.

5. Don't forget to celebrate your success and recognize everyone who lent support. If you are presenting an exhibition, use the Dream-Makers "helpers" certificate (which you can download from Crayola.com/dreammakers), or make your own.

6. Assess results. What are your "lessons learned"?

Your Own Exhibition

Publicly exhibiting their art is one of the most exciting and rewarding gifts you can give your students. Having an exhibition opening is a wonderful way to engage the school, parents, and community, especially if members of different groups help plan and put on the event. Here are some suggestions for a successful experience:

- Always display all students' work that was generated by the Dream-Makers® activities.

- Exhibit artwork in a way that honors the students.

- Matting the artwork can be simple and inexpensive. For ideas on mounting and exhibiting artwork, go to Crayola.com/successguide.

- Consider displaying the students' dream statements along with the work. These can be especially compelling for adults viewing the work.

- You can demonstrate the value of your program by displaying the standards the lesson addressed with the artwork.

- If you select art to submit to the national program, develop selection criteria based on your school's or district's guidelines for assessment.

- For your opening, enlist the help of parents and local businesses. Serve child-friendly refreshments and have a simple ceremony/photo op for presenting certificates of recognition to students and helpers. Invite district and community leaders so you can showcase their support.

About Crayola® Dream-Makers®

Mathematics in Art History

Math and art have harmonized virtually from prehistory. The earliest paintings and carvings are often related to calendars and the tracking of celestial events, such as full moons. There are many examples of mathematical themes, designs, tricks, and even proofs being expressed in works of art.

Well-known examples include the geometric figures and "magic square" found in **Albrecht Durer's** woodcut *Melancholia I*; the **Golden Rectangle** as an organizing principle in architecture and painting; and the geometric discipline known as **perspective**, which helps artists depict three-dimensional space on a two-dimensional surface. More modern examples of mathematical principles in art are the works of **M.C. Escher** and various contemporary artists working with **fractal** images.

Of course, visual art is an essential component of some branches of mathematics, notably geometry. Visual representations (drawing or sculpture), help mathematicians communicate proofs of the **Pythagorean Theorem** and show properties of the **Platonic Solids**. In fact, one of the earliest proofs of the Pythagorean Theorem is an illustration in the Chinese treatise *Zhoubi suanjing*, the original of which may date back to 400-200 BCE.

Crayola Dream-Makers is the national program that encourages Kindergarten through 6th grade children's creative development and learning, recognizes student artists, and displays children's artwork in a national exhibition. Since 1984, millions of students and thousands of art and classroom teachers have participated in the program. The program has been recognized by the U.S. Department of Education, the John F. Kennedy Center for the Performing Arts, the National Association of Elementary School Principals, the Association of Children's Museums, the National Art Education Association and other leading arts and education organizations.

Since its inception, the program has collected 3,300 works of art by children, which are professionally framed and matted, documented, used as teaching tools, and exhibited to advocate for art education. A large part of the collection decorates the offices of the U.S. Department of Education in Washington, D.C. To view children's artwork from past years of the program, log on to Crayola.com/dreammakers and visit the Gallery of Children's Art.

Mastering Math Concepts Through Visual Art

An additional benefit to the Dream-Makers approach is the pleasure that children get from demonstrating mastery in a visual or tactile way. This is confirmed by art teacher Elyse Martin and fifth grade math teacher Trish Davlantes, who tested *The Average Time —You See!* with their students from the Michael Jordan Community School in Chicago. They told us how much their students enjoyed learning about averaging while creating sketchbooks in this lesson. Their students recorded the time it took to see and make drawings, then thoroughly analyzed the data for both individual and aggregate results. Their exuberant results illustrate the lesson on pages 28 – 29.

How to Use Dream-Makers®

This guide is the heart of the Dream-Makers program. It contains 12 classroom-tested lesson plans based on National Visual Art Standards and the Principles and Standards for School Mathematics from the National Council of Teachers of Mathematics. It is a complete resource that provides curriculum-related activities, background information, examples of children's artwork, and museum images that give cultural and historical context to lessons. Supplementary material is available online at Crayola.com/dreammakers.

Each lesson is complete, containing step-by-step instructions, material lists, classroom time, extensions, alternatives, and references to the applicable standards. They may be followed verbatim, adapted, or used as a springboard for your own lessons. In this edition of the guide, we have incorporated suggestions for collaboration between classroom teachers and art teachers, although an individual art or classroom teacher may easily present the lessons.

Exploring the additional resources—such as books or websites listed under Resources with various lessons—can enhance learning. In addition, teachers can use the art images in this guide as a starting point for discussions about history, world cultures or materials, patterns, textures and other formal qualities of handmade objects.

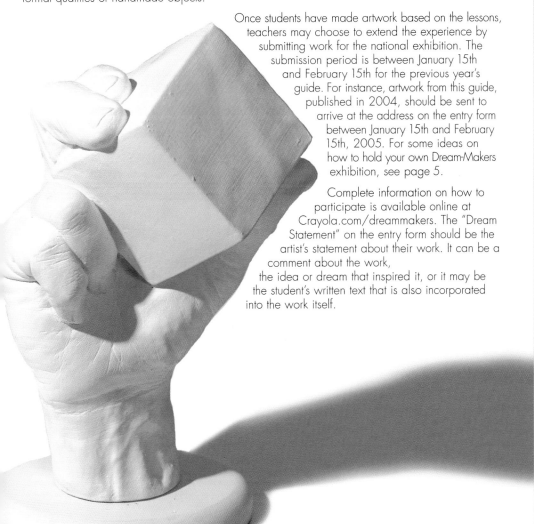

Once students have made artwork based on the lessons, teachers may choose to extend the experience by submitting work for the national exhibition. The submission period is between January 15th and February 15th for the previous year's guide. For instance, artwork from this guide, published in 2004, should be sent to arrive at the address on the entry form between January 15th and February 15th, 2005. For some ideas on how to hold your own Dream-Makers exhibition, see page 5.

Complete information on how to participate is available online at Crayola.com/dreammakers. The "Dream Statement" on the entry form should be the artist's statement about their work. It can be a comment about the work, the idea or dream that inspired it, or it may be the student's written text that is also incorporated into the work itself.

Dream-Makers on the Web

Crayola.com/dreammakers has been significantly expanded with supplementary material for the program and the guide.

Features include:

- Additional material for each lesson – extensions, adaptations, content webs, and links to resources

- Dream-Makers guides past and present

- Printable certificates for recognizing children's participation and adults' support

- Thousands of images of children's Dream-Makers art from the last 20 years

- More information about our Educational Alliances

- How to order guides

- And much more!

Consider developing your own curriculum webs, aligned with your school board-approved curricula. Your district Curriculum Coordinator or Supervisor can help you align lessons with your school's educational goals.

National Visual Arts Standards

Below are Content Standards from the voluntary National Visual Arts Standards, and a brief synopsis of the corresponding Achievement Standards. Though many educators are well acquainted with these, they are included here for easy reference. While these standards have not been adopted in full by each state, most state standards correspond with National Standards or contain the essence of them.

For information about the complete standards book, which includes a useful introduction and rationale for each age group, call the National Art Education Association at 1-800-299-8321, or visit their website at www.naea-reston.org.

Content Standards	Achievement Standards Synopsis for Grades K-4 & 5-8	
1. Understanding and applying media, techniques, and processes	In K-4, students recognize various materials, techniques and processes, and can describe and use these to communicate ideas, experiences, and stories, and to elicit viewer response. In K-8, students use materials and tools safely.	In 5-8, students select media, techniques and processes to enhance communication, then analyze whether or not these choices were effective, and reflect on the reasons.
2. Using knowledge of structures and functions	In K-4, students recognize different ways visual characteristics, expressive features and organizational principles communicate ideas and elicit different responses.	In 5-8, students generalize about the effects of visual structures and functions of art, use these to improve their own work's communication potential, and reflect upon whether or not these uses were effective.
3. Choosing and evaluating a range of subject matter, symbols and ideas	In K-4, students explore and understand prospective content for their art, then select and use appropriate subjects, symbols and ideas to make art meaningful.	In 5-8, students integrate concepts with content to communicate intended meaning as they work, using subjects, themes, and symbols that demonstrate knowledge of their work's contexts, values and aesthetics.
4. Understanding the visual arts in relation to history and cultures	In K-4, students understand that visual arts and specific artworks have a history and identifiable relationship to various cultures, times and places, and that time, place, culture and art influence each other.	In 5-8, students identify, describe, and compare characteristics of select artworks from various eras and cultures; identify the works' places along a cultural timeline; relate how time/place influence a work's visual characteristics.
5. Reflecting upon and assessing the characteristics and merits of their work and the work of others	In K-4, students understand/describe purposes for creating artworks, how people's experiences influence a work, how various viewers' responses to one work differ.	In 5-8, students compare purposes for creating works; analyze a specific work's meaning by reviewing its history/culture; describe and compare responses to their own artworks and responses to works of other eras/cultures.
6. Making connections between visual arts and other disciplines	In K-4, students understand/use similarities and differences between visual arts and other arts disciplines. They find connections between visual arts and other subjects.	In 5-8, students compare characteristics of works in two or more art forms that share similar subject matter, eras, or cultural context. They describe the interrelationships between art and the principles/subject matter of other disciplines.

To learn more about art education's impact on children's development and learning, the Arts Education Partnership has published the following resources:

- *Critical Links – Learning in the Arts and Student Academic and Social Development* (2002). This compendium summarizes and discusses 62 research studies that examine the effects of arts learning on students' social and academic skills.

- *Champions of Change – The Impact of the Arts on Learning* (1999). This report compiles seven major studies that provide evidence of enhanced learning and achievement when students are involved in a variety of arts experiences.

These resources are available on the Arts Education Partnership's website at www.aep-arts.org.

Standards for School Mathematics

Number and Operations Standard

Instructional programs from prekindergarten through grade 12 should enable all students to—

- understand numbers, ways of representing numbers, relationships among numbers, and number systems;
- understand meanings of operations and how they relate to one another;
- compute fluently and make reasonable estimates.

Algebra Standard

Instructional programs from prekindergarten through grade 12 should enable all students to—

- understand patterns, relations, and functions;
- represent and analyze mathematical situations and structures using algebraic symbols;
- use mathematical modes to represent and understand quantitative relationships;
- analyze change in various contexts.

Geometry Standard

Instructional programs from prekindergarten through grade 12 should enable all students to—

- analyze characteristics and properties of two- and three-dimensional geometric shapes and develop mathematical arguments about geometric relationships;
- specify locations and describe spatial relationships using coordinate geometry and other representational systems;
- apply transformations and use symmetry to analyze mathematical situations;
- use visualization, spatial reasoning, and geometric modeling to solve problems.

Measurement Standard

Instructional programs from prekindergarten through grade 12 should enable all students to—

- understand measurable attributes of objects and the units, systems, and processes of measurement;
- apply appropriate techniques, tools, and formulas to determine measurements.

Data Analysis and Probability Standard

Instructional programs from prekindergarten through grade 12 should enable all students to—

- formulate questions that can be addressed with data and collect, organize, and display relevant data to answer them;
- select and use appropriate statistical methods to analyze data;
- develop and evaluate inferences and predictions that are based on data;
- understand and apply basic concepts of probability.

Problem Solving Standard

Instructional programs from prekindergarten through grade 12 should enable all students to—

- build new mathematical knowledge through problem solving;
- solve problems that arise in mathematics and in other contexts;
- apply and adapt a variety of appropriate strategies to solve problems;
- monitor and reflect on the process of mathematical problem solving.

Reasoning and Proof Standard

Instructional programs from prekindergarten through grade 12 should enable all students to—

- recognize reasoning and proof as fundamental aspects of mathematics;
- make and investigate mathematical conjectures;
- develop and evaluate mathematical arguments and proofs;
- select and use various types of reasoning and methods of proof.

Communication Standard

Instructional programs from prekindergarten through grade 12 should enable all students to—

- organize and consolidate their mathematical thinking through communication;
- communicate their mathematical thinking coherently and clearly to peers, teachers, and others;
- analyze and evaluate the mathematical thinking and strategies of others;
- use the language of mathematics to express mathematical ideas precisely.

Connections Standard

Instructional programs from prekindergarten through grade 12 should enable all students to—

- recognize and use connections among mathematical ideas;
- understand how mathematical ideas interconnect and build on one another to produce a coherent whole;
- recognize and apply mathematics in contexts outside of mathematics.

Representation Standard

Instructional programs from prekindergarten through grade 12 should enable all students to—

- create and use representations to organize, record and communicate mathematical ideas;
- select, apply and translate among mathematical representations to solve problems;
- use representations to model and interpret physical, social and mathematical phenomena.

Counting on a Spectacular Garden

Grade Level
K-2

Classroom Time
One to two 40-min. periods

Materials/Tools
for 24-30 students

- 30 sheets 12" x 18" colored construction paper
- 30 sheets 9" x 12" colored construction paper
- Crayola® Construction Paper™ crayons
- Textured materials (see step #3)
- Crayola School Glue
- Crayola Scissors

Tips
Place textured objects on smooth tabletop surface to achieve best-textured rubbing results. Press hard with crayon to reveal color textures.

Resources
Freight Train by Donald Crews
Rooster's Off to See the World by Eric Carle

The Glass Flowers at Harvard by Richard Evans Schultes & William A. Davis

The Art of Eric Carle by Eric Carle

Planting a Rainbow by Lois Ehlert

Rocket Minds™: Slide 'n Solve Math (age 6+); *Time Machine* (age 6+); *Think-ama-Jink Checkers* (age 6+); *Math 4 Kicks* (age 6+)

Blaschka Glass Models of Plants, reproductions, pp. 44-45

Floral Textile reproduction, p. 47

Objective
Children create garden collages depicting colorful flowers growing in beds. They count the garden flowers with understanding and recognize how many are contained in sets of objects.

Teacher Preparation
Classroom Teacher: Draw a picture showing a box with three circles inside and two circles outside. Guide children to make up sentences identifying how many circles they count in total, and how many are in sets inside and outside the box. Use more circles as needed to stretch children's math skills.

Art Teacher: Collect visual examples of different types of flowers. Find pictures of gardens that contain spectacular flowers and plants growing in multiple beds.

Discussion Starters
Classroom Teacher: Read the book *Rooster's Off to See the World* to students. Stop when the animals must decide where to spend the night. Tell children to pretend there are two small sheds. How many animals would they put into each shed? Ask several children to explain how they grouped the animals and how many are in each group.

Art Teacher: Ask students to recall what they did when they heard the story *Rooster's Off to See the World*. Show students examples of gardens with multiple beds. Ask children to create a collage depicting two gardens separated by a fence or other garden accessories. After they create the collage, they count and compare the number of flowers in the beds.

Process
1. Fold construction paper in half so the short ends meet. Crease the fold and then open the paper flat. Draw a garden divided in two by the fold. Consider drawing fence posts, scarecrows, or a birdhouse as a divider between the two flowerbeds (sides of the paper).
2. Look at photographs of various types of flowers. Choose colors and shapes that are appealing.
3. Create construction paper rubbings. Place paper on top of flat textural materials such as leaves, plastic sink mats, very coarse sandpaper, screens, netting, or latch hook mats. Rub over the paper with the side of an unwrapped crayon. Press hard to achieve dramatic color effects in flower designs.
4. Cut out flower shapes from the decorated paper and glue blossoms inside both beds divided by a garden fixture. Explore creating new species of flowers that are not known to science.
5. Draw flower elements such as stems and leaves. Consider adding other garden objects on each side of the divided drawing.
6. Outline blossom shapes so the design can be seen from a distance.

Assessment
Have children summarize their learning. Children count the number of spectacular flowers they drew in both beds, and write the numerals on their drawings. Check that the total count of flowers matches the drawings. Ask children to write sentences that describe various math facts about their flowers and flower beds.

Visual Arts Standard 3

Mathematics Standards
Number and Operations
Problem Solving

Artwork by students from Little River
Elementary School, Durham, NC.
Teachers: Barbi Bailey-Smith, Carly Doughty, Janice House

Background Information

In April 1887 a spectacular marvel occurred. A shipment of 20 glass flowers arrived in New York City from Dresden, Germany. The flowers were the first of 847 life-size glass models of flowers that were created and shipped to Harvard University in Cambridge, Massachusetts. Two German artists, Leopold Blaschka and his son, Rudolf, created these garden marvels that included models of plants, flowers, and other botanical objects.

The glass flowers are used mostly as teaching tools for students studying the plant sciences at Harvard. In addition to being stunningly accurate to the smallest detail, these spectacular wonders are in bloom all year. The Ware Collection of Glass Models of Plants, as the collection is known, is housed in two rooms on the third floor of the Botanical Museum of Harvard University.

In the Face of Symmetry

Grade Level
K-2

Classroom Time
One to two 40-min. periods

Materials/Tools
for 24-30 students
- 30 sheets 12" x 18" white drawing paper
- Crayola® Artista II® Tempera paint, 1 pint each of red, yellow, blue, black, brown, peach, violet; 1 quart of white
- Crayola Overwriters® Markers
- Crayola Paint Brushes
- Crayola Washable Markers Classpack®, conical tip
- Paper towels
- Sponges
- Water containers

Tips
Encourage children to experiment with loading the brush so they have enough paint to make substantial shapes, but not so much that strokes are hard to control.

Resources
Triangle, Square, Circle
  by William Wegman

When Pigasso Met Mootisse
  by Nina Laden

Rocket Minds™: Slide 'n Solve Math (age 6+); *Time Machine* (age 6+); *Think-ama-Jink Checkers* (age 6+); *Math 4 Kicks* (age 6+)

Woman, Joan Miró, reproduction p. 35

Objective
Children identify shapes and design a face that demonstrates symmetry.

Teacher Preparation

Classroom Teacher: Read the book *Triangle, Square, Circle* to students. Identify and make a list of all the shapes children can find in the classroom.

Art Teacher: Collect reproductions of artifacts that illustrate both symmetrical and asymmetrical composition. Cut out assorted paper shapes. Draw lines down the middle of shapes to illustrate symmetry and asymmetry.

Discussion Starters

Classroom Teacher: Ask questions such as: Who can name some basic shapes? What do those shapes look alike? What happens to a shape when you divide the shape by drawing a line (line of symmetry) down its middle (or fold it in half)? Is the shape the same on each half? Explain that symmetrical shapes are identical in size, form, and position on both sides. Another way to describe these shapes is to call them congruent. Shapes that are not identical on both sides are called asymmetrical shapes.

Art Teacher: With students, look at reproductions of art created by Joan Miró and Alexander Calder. Ask students to pretend that they see a line drawn down the middle of some of the shapes in the art (or imagine the shapes are folded in half). Are the shapes symmetrical or asymmetrical?

Process

1. Fold drawing paper in half. Crease the fold and then open the paper flat.
2. Draw a line along the fold with a Crayola Overwriters Under Color Marker.
3. Paint a variety of shapes on one side of the fold. Experiment with loading just the right amount of paint on the brush to apply it to paper in a controlled way.
4. While the paint is still wet, fold paper closed. Press down gently with palm and fingers. Be careful not to push paint beyond the edge of the folded paper.
5. Open the paper flat. Observe the shapes in the painted designs. Are the two sides of the paper asymmetrical or symmetrical? How do you know? Air-dry.
6. Study the position of the painted shapes. Search for a face revealed among the shapes. Fill areas around the shapes with Overwriters Under Color Markers to embellish and strengthen the face concept. Add details with Over Color Markers to extend creative possibilities.

Assessment
Have children summarize what they learned. Ask children to accurately identify symmetrical and asymmetrical shapes their classmates created.

Visual Arts Standard 2
Mathematics Standards
  Algebra
  Reasoning and Proof

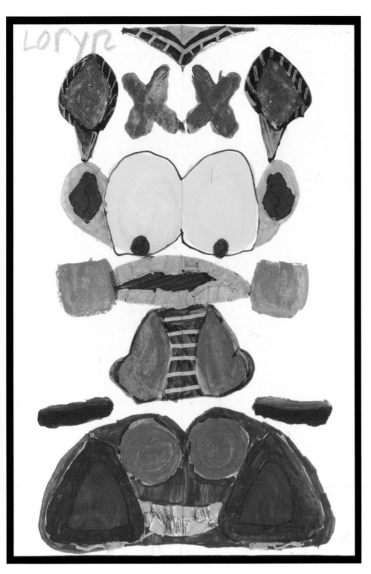

Artwork by students from Foothills Elementary
School, Colorado Springs, CO.
Teachers: Kay La Bella, Karen Sommerfeld

Background Information

Alexander Calder, "Sandy" to his friends, was born near Philadelphia,
Pennsylvania, to a family of artists. When Sandy was only five years old, he
made little wood and wire people and animals, and at eight he made jewelry
for his sister Peggy's doll. Sandy always liked to think of new contraptions. In the
fourth grade he made a blotting pad to hang on the side of his desk. He invent-
ed many new and playful ways to make sculpture, including portraits out of wire;
hanging, moving "mobiles;" and giant standing steel "stabiles." Many of the
shapes observed in his art illustrate asymmetry.

Joan Miró was born in 1893 in Barcelona, Spain, in a region known as
Catalonia. He began to make art at the age of eight. As a young man, a
serious illness ended his career as a bookkeeper and contributed to his decision
to dedicate himself to painting. Like other artists of the early twentieth century
he was drawn to Paris, France, where he met many other important artists.
His art is marked by his use of expressive colors, lines and large shapes, often
arranged on a simple background, conveying a dreamlike atmosphere. He
always stayed close to his Catalan roots, and he often incorporated in his
work the people, places and folk art images of his native land. Like Calder,
many of the shapes observed in Miró's art depict asymmetry.

Gee's-ometric Wisdom

Grade Level
K-2

Classroom Time
One or two 40-min. periods

Materials/Tools
for 24-30 Students

- 30 sheets white drawing paper, cut into 9" squares
- 120 4" paper squares
- Crayola® Colored Pencils
- Crayola Overwriters® Markers Classpack®
- Crayola School Glue
- Crayola Scissors

Tip
Cover work surface with newspaper when coloring shapes.

Resources
Shapes, Shapes, Shapes by Tana Hoban

The Quilts of Gee's Bend by John Beardsley, William Arnett, Pauljane Arnett, & Jane Livingston

Rocket Minds™: Slide 'n Solve Math (age 6+); *Time Machine* (age 6+); *Think-ama-Jink Checkers* (age 6+); *Math 4 Kicks* (age 6+)

Gee's Bend Quilt reproductions, p. 34

Objective
Children analyze, assemble, and describe relationships among geometric shapes. Students develop math arguments about geometric relationships in a quilt design they create.

Teacher Preparation
Classroom Teacher: Find and display a quilt or pictures of quilts. Cut out simple shapes such as rectangles, squares, triangles, circles, ovals, and a rhombus. Display them around the quilt.

Art Teacher: Cut 4-inch paper squares and 9-inch drawing paper squares for the class. Create a model for children that shows how to combine two triangles to make a square. Prepare decorative papers to show students how they can arrange triangles to extend square designs with the decorative papers they make. Consider using scrap paper saved from other projects, just as the quilters of Gee's Bend make stunning works of art from recycled cloth *(see background information)*.

Discussion Starters
Classroom Teacher: How do you think we can use shapes to make new shapes? Who can put two triangles together to make a square? How could you make a figure 8 with circles? If you put a lot of squares in a line you can create a very long rectangle.

Art Teacher: What have you learned about combining shapes to create new shapes? What were some of the new shapes you made? Quilt artists are geometric geniuses. They are always thinking about geometry and how they can combine shapes to create new quilt patterns.

Process
Divide squares into triangles of different sizes

1. Start with a 4-inch paper square. Fold square diagonally.
2. Cut along the fold to create two triangles.
3. Fold triangles in half and cut along fold.
4. Repeat the process to create proportionally smaller triangles with which to create smaller squares.

Design with triangles to create square patterns

1. Each child takes three more 4-inch paper squares.
2. Fill one side of the paper squares with decorative lines, shapes, and colors using Overwriters Under Color and Over Color Markers.
3. Cut decorative paper into triangles. Arrange triangles so they reveal new decorative squares. Allow time to explore solutions. Encourage children to think about, position, and reposition triangles to create unusual designs.
4. Settle on a final design. Glue the triangles on drawing paper squares.

Assessment
Ask children to summarize what they learned. Have children use colored pencils to draw and write a paragraph describing what they learned about combining their decorative shapes. Invite children to share their responses and list their ideas on a chart. Discuss what they still want to find out about combining shapes.

Visual Arts Standard 6
Mathematics Standards
  Geometry
  Communication

Artwork by students from T.J. Lee Elementary School, Irving, TX.
Teacher: Jennifer Parks

Background Information

People have created quilts for the useful purpose of keeping folks covered and warm. But quilts can also be things of beauty. The women of Gee's Bend—a small, remote, community in rural Alabama—have created hundreds of quilt masterpieces dating from the early 20th century to the present.

They work with used, discarded, or rejected bits of cloth and follow linear patterns that combine shape and color, often with the flavor of the African textile traditions handed down from their ancestors. Quilts are products of everyday life, mental agility, deep sensitivity, and geometric genius.

Patterns of Love Beads

Grade Level
K-2

Classroom Time
Two or three 40-min. periods

Materials/Tools
for 24-30 students

- Clear adhesive tape
- Cotton cord or heavy string, cut in 36" lengths
- Crayola® Model Magic®– colors and white
- Crayola Scissors
- Crayola Washable Markers Classpack, conical tip
- Crayola Washable Watercolors
- Crayola Watercolor Brushes
- Plastic drinking straws
- Pony beads (available from most craft stores)

Tip
Cut plastic straw pieces so they extend beyond the ends of the modeled beads. Trim flush after bead has dried.

Resources
A Universal Aesthetic, Collectible Beads by Robert K. Liu

Rocket Minds™: Slide 'n Solve Math (ages 6+); Time Machine (ages 6+); Think-ama-Jink Checkers (ages 6+); Math 4 Kicks (ages 6+)

Visual Arts Standard 1
Mathematics Standards
Measurement
Connections

Objective

Children create 1960s hippie-like necklaces containing three-dimensional geometric beads. They compare and order the beads according to patterns.

Teacher Preparation

Classroom Teacher: Think of groups of words that are associated with a pattern or cycle, such as the seasons of the year or the water cycle. Write each word on an individual strip of paper, large enough for the whole class to see. Be prepared to display words during your discussion.

Art Teacher: Cut plastic straws into 1-inch pieces so that each child will have about 20. Children may enjoy assisting with this task. Using Model Magic in a variety of colors, form the following marble-size geometric forms: sphere, cube, rectangular prism, cone, pyramid, and egg-shape. String the beads in patterns of forms and colors. Find images or reproductions of hippie-era necklaces that support patterning for display.

Discussion Starters

Classroom Teacher: Who knows what a cycle is? What are some examples? Can you say at least two repetitions of a cycle? For example: spring, summer, fall, winter, spring, summer, fall, winter; or morning, afternoon, evening, night, morning, afternoon, evening, night. Can you think of your own repetitions?

Art Teacher: In class you learned about repetition and cycles. When artists use repetition and cycles in their art they repeat designs or forms. A good example of this is bead necklaces that some of your parents or grandparents may have worn in the 1960s. In those days, these necklaces were called hippie or love beads. Today we're going to learn about patterns and cycles and create some fun hippie-bead necklaces.

Process

Create the beads

1. Select a marble-size amount of white or colored Model Magic.
2. Wrap the Model Magic around a 1-inch piece of plastic straw.
3. Shape the modeling material so that it forms a bead in one of the following forms: sphere, cone, cylinder, cube, rectangular prism, pyramid, or egg.
4. Make four or more of every type of bead form.
5. Add color by drawing on the beads with washable markers. Or paint dried beads with watercolors.

Design the necklace

1. Sort similar beads into piles.
2. String beads on cotton cord. Create patterns to show understanding of cycle and repetition. Use pony beads to separate Model Magic beads if desired.
3. Tape the cord ends together. Close adult supervision is essential whenever children wear anything around their necks.
4. Encourage children to show their creations to people who might have worn similar beads in the 60s!

Assessment

Children summarize what they learned. Ask children to create a class chart to illustrate their patterns. Challenge children to look for and identify different cycles and patterns designed into their hippie-bead necklaces. Assign one column per student. Ask students to check each other's patterns for repetitive cycles.

Artwork by students from Spring Garden
Elementary School, Bethlehem, PA.
Teacher: Pat Check

Background Information

About 40,000 years ago, human beings were making and using beads. Within the last 30 years, archaeologists and anthropologists began to take notice of beads and their importance to people and their lives. In an article in *Lapidary Journal*, Lynda McDaniel writes that "beads were among humans' earliest expression of abstract ideas. Although not functional in the sense of a tool or a weapon, beads carry strong symbolic significance."

In the late 1960's, young people used necklaces of "love beads" to show their rejection of violence and their hopes for peace, reflecting the mood of the times. Although both men and women wear necklaces today, in the 1960's, young men who wore love beads were making a daring social statement of protest against war and desire for universal fellowship. These necklaces were often handmade and exchanged as signs of love and friendship.

A Bountiful Table- Sharing Fairly

Grade Level
3-4

Classroom Time
One or two 40-min. periods

Materials/Tools
for 24-30 students
- 30 sheets 12" x 18" white drawing paper
- Crayola® Erasable Colored Pencils (6 packages)
- Crayola Gel FX Markers
- Crayola Oil Pastels
- Crayola Scissors
- Erasers
- Overhead transparencies
- Paper plates
- Paper towels
- Recycled file folders

Tip
Shake off pastel crumbs into trash before cutting drawings into slices.

Resources
The National Gallery of Art website: ww.nga.org (search "Thiebaud")

Wayne Thiebaud Paintings at The National Gallery of Art, Washington, DC

Rocket Minds™: Spin, Spend, and Earn (ages 8+); *Think-ama-Jink Checkers* (age 6+)

Cakes, Wayne Thiebaud, reproduction, p. 48

Objective
Students create drawings of food to reflect their understanding of fractions by informally exploring the concept of equal or fair shares.

Teacher Preparation

Classroom Teacher: Draw and cut various sizes of circles from recycled file folders and cut them into halves, quarters, and eighths. Cut more full circles for each student to use in class. Children can assist with this if they finish other activities early.

Art Teacher: Collect and display cake paintings by Wayne Thiebaud on your class bulletin board. Gather Crayola Gel FX Markers and several clear overhead transparencies.

Discussion Starters

Classroom Teacher: What does sharing mean to you? What do we mean when we share fairly? Who has ever cut a cake or pizza into slices? When you take a whole cake and cut it into pieces, you are dividing one thing into several pieces. If you have three people and one whole cake, how can you divide the cake so that every person gets a fair share? Let's use your paper cake shapes to see how we can divide one circle fairly so that each person gets a fair share. What healthier foods could you choose instead of cake that also could be divided into sections? (large fruits such as watermelon, fruit pizza, baked potato, loaf of bread)

Art Teacher: Let's review what you learned in class about sharing fairly. How would you divide a loaf of bread for three people? For two? For four? For the whole class?

Place a clear transparency on top of an image of a loaf of bread. Ask a student to use a Crayola Gel FX Marker as if it were a knife to "cut" the bread into slices. Wipe off markers to repeat the process with another student. Invite students to create oil pastel drawings that illustrate a table filled with cakes and pies (or more healthy foods). Divide children into small groups of three to seven students (odd numbers will be more challenging). They will divide their desserts so that there are enough pieces to serve everyone in their small group. For an even greater challenge, ask more advanced students to divide ALL the desserts on the page so that everyone in the class gets an equal amount.

Process

1. Ask students to think of their paper as if it were the top of a table. Visualize looking down onto a table filled with cakes, pies, cookies, and other desserts (or healthier foods such as pizza or fruit).
2. Fill drawing paper with erasable colored pencil line drawings of foods seen from above. Divide foods so each child in the group would receive an equal share of each item on their table.
3. Exchange drawings with classmates to check for drawing accuracy. Erase lines if needed for accuracy.
4. Fill completed line drawings with oil pastel color. Decorate them with designs you might find on fancy desserts.
5. Cut designs into slices if desired.

Assessment

Encourage children to summarize what they learned. Students exchange dessert-table drawings and check that shares are accurate and fair. If drawings are cut in slices, pile up slices to see whether they match exactly.

Visual Arts Standard 5
Mathematics Standards
Data Analysis and Probability
Representation

Quote

Although the lesson focused on dividing into fair shares, third graders were involved in several math concepts in the process. Working in collaborative groups, they estimated amounts and size relationships, as well as informally investigating the division process with several methods of cutting the cakes. One third grader summed up the lesson by stating that "art is just like math, you have to know both to get it right".
—*Lynn Schatzle, Wood Creek Elementary School, Farmington Hills, MI*

Artwork by students from Wood Creek Elementary School, Farmington Hills, MN.
Teacher: Lynn Schatzel

Background Information

Wayne Thiebaud is perhaps best known for his still-life paintings of everyday objects, especially his painterly depictions of cakes and pies. Although closely associated with the Pop Art movement of the 1960's, Thiebaud's subjects reflect a sense of nostalgia and reverence in contrast to the more ironic images of modern American consumerism in much Pop Art.

While most Pop Artists were reducing the nuances of touch in their work, Thiebaud exploited the physical properties of paint to capture the look and feel of the substance depicted. Thiebaud described this palpable, sensuous employment of paint as "object transference."

Whimsical Charting and Checking

Grade Level
3-4

Classroom Time
Two or three 40-min. periods

Materials/Tools
for 24-30 students
- Crayola® Colored Pencils Classpack®
- Crayola Glitter Glue (optional)
- Crayola Model Magic®
- Crayola School Glue
- Crayola Scissors
- Ribbon, yarn, or string
- White paper

Tips
Apply glue over modeled cushion-like form to help attach and secure beads to the form.

Resources
Basic Beadwork for Beginners
by Mitsuko Muto

Geckos & Other Bead Animals
by Drew Wilkens

Rocket Minds™: Spin, Spend, and Earn (ages 8+); Think-ama-Jink Checkers (ages 6+)

Beaded Whimsey reproductions, pp. 38-39

Objective

Students create a beaded pin cushion-like 3-D form reflective of artifacts known as "Beaded Whimsies" to learn about charting, estimating and checking data.

Teacher Preparation

Classroom Teacher: Create a chart with one column for each student and rows marked by colored beads. Title the chart Charting, Estimating and Checking Beaded Whimsies. Ask students to assist in making the chart or create a reproducible chart.

Art Teacher: Create 20 to 30 smaller than pea-size spheres of colored Model Magic. Air-dry overnight. Create a simple cushion-like three-dimensional form with Model Magic. Embed a ribbon hanger. Air-dry overnight. Cut 30 or more 3 x 4-inch rectangles from white paper.

Discussion Starters

Classroom Teacher: What are some ways to keep track of numerical data? For example, how could you record the number of colored beads it takes you to cover a small space? You can use a chart to record estimates and tell how many of each bead you used to create your art. After each student estimates the number of beads used against the actual beads used, we can calculate the total number of beads used by our entire class.

Art Teacher: Some Native Americans created beaded pincushion whimsies that they sold to the tourists. Maybe they charted how many beads they needed for each whimsy to help plan their designs. Charting data helps us understand complex number operations. Let's estimate, count and record the different numbers of Model Magic beads it takes to create your beaded whimsies.

Process

1. Draw a simple shape (star, heart, shell) on a 3 x 4-inch paper rectangle using colored pencils.
2. Draw a second basic shape inside the original shape. Create a 2-D bead-like pattern inside the design by filling the drawing with very small color-filled circles next to each other. Use this as your pattern.
3. Create a cushion-like three-dimensional form with a tennis-ball amount of Model Magic reflective of the simple shape you drew.
4. Cut one 10"-long piece of ribbon and tie ends. Poke the end of the ribbon circle or paper clip deep into the top of the moist modeled form with a colored pencil point. Smooth inserted area with fingers.
5. Roll smaller than pea-size colored spheres from Model Magic.
6. Glue the pea-sized forms to the simple form, filling it to reflect the pattern in your 2-D design. Air-dry the whimsy overnight.
7. Apply glitter glue to form for dramatic sparkle effects.
8. Estimate the number of beads in the design, then count and record the number of each color of beads needed to create each whimsy on a class chart.

Assessment

Have students summarize what they learned. Students count each other's beads and resolve any differences. Record all findings on the class chart, using different colors in each column to obtain individual totals. Students compile the data to determine estimates and actual total number of each color of beads, and the total number of beads created by the entire class, and report their findings.

Visual Arts Standard 4
Mathematics Standards
Number and Operations
Problem Solving

Quote

Making whimsy creations with Model Magic was a real motivation. This activity gave kids a real-world connection for using estimation and graphing concepts.
—*Jen O'Flaherty, Sandy Plains Elementary School, Baltimore, MD*

Background Information

Native American women were skilled in beadwork. To economically survive in a changing world, enterprising women of the Iroquois nation, particularly from the Mohawk and Tuscarora tribes, designed and crafted beaded items to sell to tourists in the late 1800's through early 1900's. These items, particularly pincushions, became quite popular as souvenirs at places such as Niagara Falls. "Beaded whimsies," as we now call them, were made in shapes such as hearts, canoes, and high-top shoes. Their stuffed fabric bases were embellished with seed and bugle beads in a wide array of hues. Motifs included birds, flowers, leaves, and U.S. flags. Sometimes they were emblazoned with dates and the names of travel destinations. Very few of the designs were typical of the motifs used on the Native Americans' own beaded items. Instead they were shrewdly designed to specifically appeal to the gaudy tastes of the Victorian tourists.

Counting Shapes Among the Splatter

Grade Level
3-4

Classroom Time
Two or three 40-min. periods

Materials/Tools
for 24-30 students

- 24 sheets 9" x 12" 80 lb. or heavier weight paper
- Regular paper towels
- Crayola® Glitter Glue
- Crayola Scissors
- Crayola Watercolor Colored Pencils (12 packages)
- Crayola Watercolor Brushes
- Rulers
- Sandpaper
- Spray bottles
- Water containers

Tips

- Use 80-lb. white drawing paper or an inexpensive watercolor paper of a similar or greater weight for best results.

- Use a clean spray bottle with clear water. For example, empty contents of window cleaner pump sprayer and wash thoroughly. Adjust spray nozzle for finest mist, then hold nozzle 2 to 3 feet away from paper towel surface while spraying for best results.

- Consider sharpening both ends of watercolor pencils and have extra hand-held sharpeners handy for immediate use.

- Use limited palette of pencil color to achieve non-muddy color results.

Resources
Websites with images of Paul Klee's work: *www.nga.gov, www.phila-museum.org* (search "Klee")

Klee by Norbert Lynton

Rocket Minds™: Think-ama-Jink Checkers (age 6+)

Visual Arts Standard 1
Mathematics Standards
  Algebra
  Reasoning and Proof

Objective
Students analyze shapes and patterns in compositions as they create Paul Klee-like images.

Teacher Preparation

Classroom Teacher: Create a wall poster that depicts 16 squares in 4 columns and 4 rows.

Art Teacher: Create a design that illustrates 16 splattered squares where some of the squares overlap. Find examples of art by Paul Klee to display.

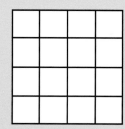

Discussion Starters

Classroom Teacher: Look at the wall poster with squares. How many squares do you see in the poster? Some of you may see 16 squares. Can anyone see more than 16? (Ask students to explain why they do or do not see more than 16 squares.) What is the biggest square you can find? How many squares can you find now? Why do you think most people would only count 16 squares?

Art Teacher: In class you found that if you looked at squares from a different perspective you could change the way you think and reason. If you look at a figure carefully, sometimes you can find geometric shapes and patterns that others may not see. Let's look at some art by Paul Klee and observe the shapes and patterns. Looking carefully often sharpens your thinking and may assist you in solving simple problems.

Process

1. Measure and cut several geometric shapes from paper towels.
2. Brush an even coat of water on heavy weight paper. Place paper towel shapes on wet paper so shapes lay flat.
3. Sand watercolor pencil color over the towel atop wet surface. Sand several colors. Do not remove shapes. Air-dry flat.
4. Reposition dried paper shape over art. Spray a very fine mist of water over the design.
5. Sand a second layer of watercolor pencil over the wet surface. Air-dry again. Display completed art.
6. Consider outlining several shapes with glitter glue to enrich surface design. Air-dry the glue.
7. Count and chart the number of shapes observed.

Assessment
Summarize findings, and have children discuss what they learned. Exchange finished designs with a partner. Partners add up the total number of shapes they see in the finished art. Check to see if their counts match.

Artwork by students from Curlew Creek
Elementary School, Palm Harbor, FL.
Teacher: Nancy Rhoads

Background Information

During the 1920's, Swiss artist Paul Klee often spattered watercolor over stencils
and netting. The effect of this technique is shown in *Glance of a Landscape*.
When Klee taught at the Bauhaus (a famous German art school), he experimented
with this technique.

In *Glance of a Landscape*, Klee applied brushstrokes of pale gray opaque watercolor on top of transparent watercolor that was spattered broadly to create trees.
Klee usually mounted his drawings on cardboard, which was where he wrote the
title and date for this composition.

Toying Around With Geometry

Grade Level
3-4

Classroom Time
One or two –40-min. periods

Materials/Tools
for 24-30 students

- Assorted strings, ribbons, yarns
- Crayola® Gel FX Markers
- Crayola Model Magic® Value Pack
- Crayola Paint Brushes
- Crayola School Glue
- Crayola Scissors
- Large paper clips
- Plastic drinking straws
- Recycled clear plastic soda bottles
- Recycled foam produce trays
- Toothpicks, buttons, feathers, or other decorative items
- Water containers
- White paper
- Wood skewers with point removed (or ⅛" dowel sticks cut in 10" lengths)

Tip
Use clean, recycled plastic food and beverage containers for supports to create functional toys.

Resources
Dolls & Toys of Native America– A Journey Through Childhood by Don & Debra McQuiston

Roarr Calder's Circus by Maira Kalman

Rocket Minds™: Think-ama-Jink Checkers (age 6+)

Vintage Toy reproductions, pp. 40-41

Visual Arts Standard 2
Mathematics Standards
Geometry
Communication

Objective
Students create a functional 3-D toy and package "insert" that reflects their spatial reasoning and communicates their thinking to others.

Teacher Preparation

Classroom Teacher: Find images of 3-D forms, including spheres, pyramids, rectangular prisms, cubes, cones, and cylinders. Encourage children to help.

Art Teacher: Create line drawings of simple 3-D forms. Ask children to help collect images of toys that illustrate combinations of simple 3-D forms they learned about in class. Ask students and their families to collect and clean clear plastic food and beverage containers for use in class.

Discussion Starters

Classroom Teacher: What shapes do you see in some of the pictures in our display? Who can find circles, triangles, rectangles, or squares? All 3-D objects are made up of combinations of 2-D flat shapes that are called planes. A cone consists of a curved triangle and circle plane. A cube is made of six equal square planes. The locations where two planes meet are called edges. Areas where three or more edges meet are called corners.

Art Teacher: Does what you see on a toy package always match what is in the box? Toys that need assembly often come with a list of parts. In class you learned about planes and 3-D forms. Here's your challenge: Create a simple toy along with a list of all the 3-D forms and planes you used to create it. This toy is for display only–not recommended for use by young children.

Process

Create the axles and wheels

1. Design a moveable toy that can be built from forms and planes. Decide how many axles the invention needs. Cut one plastic straw to about 6 inches in length for each axle.
2. Cut and insert a wooden skewer through the straw so the wood sticks out about 1 ½ inches on each end. Be careful of splinters.
3. Flatten ping-pong ball-size spheres of Model Magic into disks for wheels.
4. Push the wheels on the ends of the axles. Air-dry the wheels.

Finish the toy

1. Select a plastic bottle as the basic form (armature) for the toy. Cut out and connect additional clear plastic planes. Use Model Magic to attach pieces and extend the design of the toy beyond the armature.
2. Color the clear plastic areas of the form using Crayola Gel FX Markers.
3. Attach the axles and wheels with moist Model Magic. Use glue for more support.
4. Insert a large paper clip into Model Magic on the front of the toy. Thread a 12-inch ribbon or yarn through paper clip for a pull string.
5. Tie, twist, or glue on ribbon, toothpicks, chenille stems, and other objects for embellishment.
6. Coat the entire form for strength with a glaze of equal parts glue and water. Air-dry the toy.
7. Prepare a "Package insert," diagraming and labeling all the 3-D forms that were used to create the toy.

Assessment

Summarize learning experiences. Partners exchange toys to check package insert diagrams of planes and forms for accuracy. Name the toy and write about the process used to create the toy.

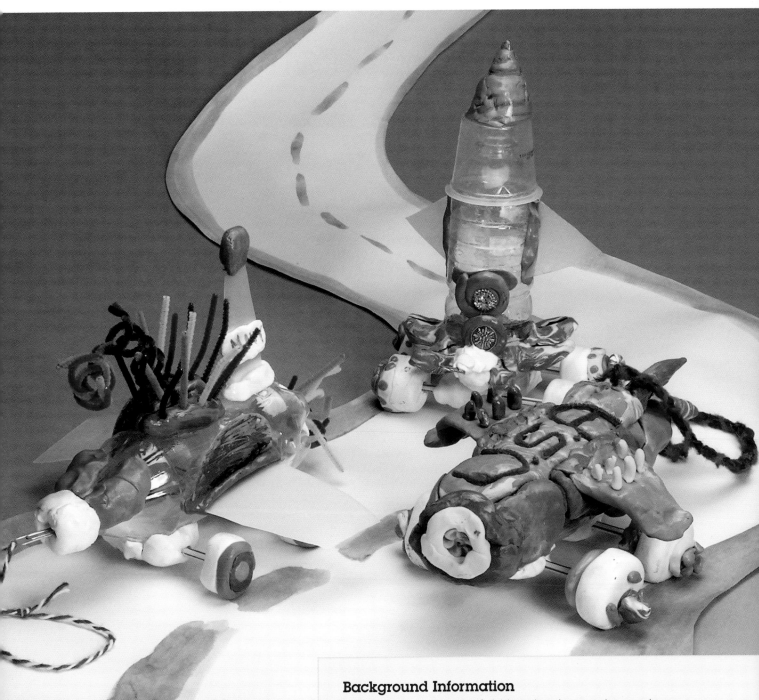

Artwork by students from John J.
Jennings Elementary School, Bristol, CT.
Teacher: Barbara Grasso

Background Information

Toys are an important part of children's lives because they stimulate young minds. Toys help children learn important concepts, develop motor and thinking skills, and express their personalities.

In many cultures, play is also a preparation for life. With Native American children, for example, each traditional toy carried a unique legacy of history, tradition, design, and practical technique. Perhaps one of the first toys, dating back to 6000 BCE, was a game of chess, which evolved from an Indian game called Chaturanga.

In Europe during the 1300's to 1500's, many toys were destroyed to eliminate the spread of the Bubonic plague. Combined with the wear and tear of time, it is difficult to find antique toys from periods before the 16th century.

Alexander Calder was fascinated by motion and created handcrafted toys early in his art career. He and other artists created forms and shapes with moveable parts. Their art, considered fun by many, moves and delights the eyes and minds of children of all ages.

Measure Twice, Create Once

Grade Level
5-6

Classroom Time
Two or three 40-min. periods

Materials/Tools
for 24-30 students

- 12" x 18" construction paper
- 5 four-cubit lengths of ribbon, yarn, or jute (optional)
- Craft paper roll
- Crayola® Construction Paper™ Crayon Classpack®
- Crayola Paint Brushes (optional)
- Crayola Premier™ Tempera, 1 pint each of red, yellow, blue, black, brown, peach, violet; 1 quart of white (optional)
- Crayola School Glue (optional)
- Rulers
- Water container (optional)
- White paper
- Yardsticks

Tip
Make careful measurement points when creating grids. Accurately align points with yardstick edge. Ask two team members to hold the yardstick securely in place while one student draws along the edge.

Resources
Math Curse
   by Jon Scieszka & Lane Smith
Picasso's One-Liners
   by Pablo Picasso
The Painter
   by Peter Catalanotto
Rocket Minds™: Think-ama-Jink Checkers (ages 6+)

Kendall Shaw painting reproductions, pp. 42-43

Visual Arts Standard 4
Mathematics Standards
   Measurement
   Connections

Objective

Children determine the real size of objects using standard units of measure, then scale up or down drawings of these objects into smaller or larger units.

Teacher Preparation

Classroom Teacher: Ask students to help create a class chart on poster board with six columns and enough rows for each child. Draw a scaled-down version of the same chart on copy paper to use as a class worksheet. Make a copy for each student.

Art Teacher: Ask students to help cut one sheet of rolled craft paper for every three to five students. Make sheets long enough to contain life-size contour drawings of a student.

Discussion Starters

Classroom Teacher: Who has measured objects using ancient Egyptian units of measure? In ancient Egypt, the main standard of length was the cubit. Who knows how long that was? A cubit was the length of a man's forearm from the elbow to the tip of the middle finger. Egyptians also used units of measure called the palm, the digit, the foot, and the span. How long do you think those were? Use a yardstick or ruler and measure the different parts of your body. Record the units of measure you observe. Compare findings to see variation.

Art Teacher: Did you ever hear the expression, Measure twice, cut once? Why is it important to measure twice when making something? How tall are you in palm units of measure? How many cubits tall are you? Measure twice to make sure. In small groups, you will figure out how to take a unit of measure and reduce or enlarge a figure contour drawing to a smaller or larger size.

Process

Draw with units of measure

1. Ask children to divide into groups of three or five.
2. Team members make a 3" or 4" grid of columns and rows of squares on brown paper using a yardstick. Number the squares from left to right. Check multiplication connections observed in numbered cells at the end of rows as they progress up or down.
3. Ask individual groups to select one child from each team to serve as a model by lying down on the paper. Ask models to move their arms and legs into unusual positions while keeping them inside the paper's border and within the grid.
4. The rest of the team traces around the model using Construction Paper Crayons.

Scale down the drawing

1. Challenge each student to figure out how to create an evenly spaced grid with the same number of rows, columns, and square cells on 12 x 18-inch construction paper, using graphite pencils. Consider lightly numbering the squares on the construction paper so they match those on the large paper for ease in visual alignment.
2. Redraw a reduced version of the figure outline on the smaller paper by carefully counting and aligning the square cells from the large drawing to the smaller drawing.
3. Fill all the shapes with Construction Paper Crayon color to enrich and personalize each drawing.
4. Encourage greater challenges and increased complexity, instruct additional models to position themselves over grid, then trace their contour before numbering squares.
5. Encourage groups to fill large group grid with tempera paint color.

Assessment

Teams summarize what they learned from this experience. Ask teams to exchange drawings and count rows and columns of shapes to check that the smaller drawing matches the larger one.

Artwork by students from Spring Garden
Elementary School, Bethlehem, PA.
Teacher: Pat Check

Background Information

Artists use the human head as the basic unit of measurement for the entire body.
The height of the head from the chin to the top of the head is the "ruler" by
which vertical lines in a human form are measured.

The width of the head is used to measure the horizontal lines in human forms.
For instance, the shoulders are about three head widths across.

Fine artists often consider that most people are 7 1/2 head lengths tall. However
when drawn to this dimension some people think the body looks short. Often
designers will stretch the length of a person in their drawing. Fashion drawings
often appear long and thin. Michaelangelo changed the proportion of his figure
sculptures to affect the way people reacted to his art.

The Average Time— You See

Grade Level
5-6

Classroom Time
One or two 40-min. periods

Materials/Tools
for 24-30 students
- 30 sheets 12" x 18" white drawing paper
- Crayola® Classic Marker Classpack®
- Crayola Fine Tip Markers Classpack®
- Crayola School Glue
- Crayola Scissors
- Stapler & staples
- White paper

Tip
Sandwich seven sheets of white paper inside a folded 12" x 18" sheet of white drawing paper. Staple along spine ½" in from the fold.

Resources
All I See
  by Cynthia Rylant & Peter Catalanotto

Latino Visions—Contemporary Chicano, Puerto Rican, and Cuban American Artists
  by James D. Cockcroft

Philadelphia Mural Project
www.muralarts.org

Mural Conservancy of Los Angeles
website: *www.lamurals.org*

Rocket Minds™: Think-ama-Jink Math Checkers (ages 6+)

Visual Arts Standard 3
Mathematics Standards
  Data Analysis and Probability

Objective
Children track the time it takes to see and draw genre drawings, and then analyze the data they collect.

Teacher Preparation

Classroom Teacher: Create a bar graph poster with markers to help children understand how to chart their drawing times.

Art Teacher: With student assistance, create sketchbooks with white drawing paper and copy paper *(see Tip)*.

Discussion Starters

Classroom Teacher: What would be the average (arithmetic mean) amount of time it would take you to create seven drawings of things you see around you? Write down your estimate. How would you calculate an average? As you draw in your sketchbooks you'll get in art class, record the time in minutes it takes you to do each daily drawing. Add the times together. Divide that number by the number of days you worked to find the average time you spent drawing.

Art Teacher: Who has seen graffiti on bridges and buildings? How long do you think it takes someone to create these blights on our communities? Fine artists take time and practice drawing in sketchbooks in preparation for creating larger works such as mural painting. Inside a seven-page sketchbook, you will create detailed drawings of objects you see in your community. Use assorted drawing materials. You may sketch objects at home and/or at school. Write down the time you start your drawing and the time you complete it at the bottom of each page. After you complete your sketchbook, you will find the average or arithmetic mean of the time you engaged in fine art drawing.

Process

1. Draw block letters to create the following title on the front cover: The Average Time— I See! by (child's name). Add interest to the cover by including shapes, color, and patterned designs along and around the letters in the title.

2. Each day, fill one page in the sketchbook with detailed crayon, marker and/or colored pencil drawings of objects seen in the environment. Mix media for added visual effects. Start by writing down the beginning drawing time on the bottom of each page. Include all details observed in the object while drawing. Finish each drawing by noting the time of completion.

3. Calculate how long it took to create each drawing.

4. Find the total amount of time it took to create all seven drawings. Divide the sum by seven to find the average (arithmetic mean) time that drawing was practiced for one week.

Assessment
Ask students to summarize what they learned. Students share sketchbooks and check for accuracy in their analyses of data collection and calculations. Ask students to resolve any math questions.

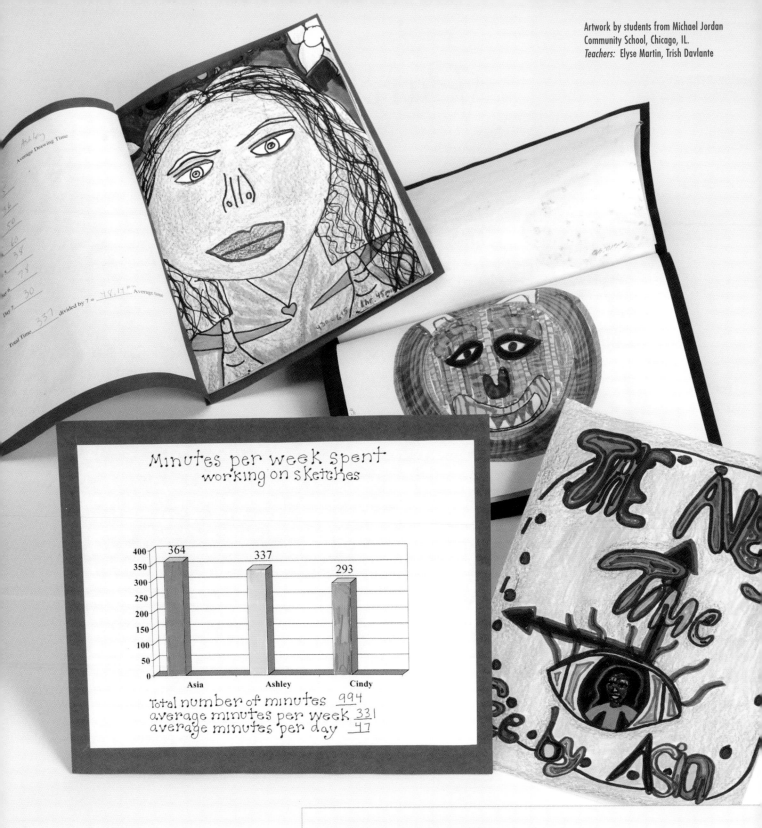

Artwork by students from Michael Jordan
Community School, Chicago, IL.
Teachers: Elyse Martin, Trish Davlante

Minutes per week spent working on sketches

Total number of minutes __994__
average minutes per week __331__
average minutes per day __47__

Quote

We were impressed with the amount of time it took to create the sketchbooks and the group mural. Calculating the time our students spent on their work elevated the importance of their art. Good art does take time! The graphs helped the visual learners grasp the averaging concept.
—*Elyse Martin, Michael Jordan Community School, Chicago, IL*

Background Information

Some art takes very little time to create and other art takes hours, weeks and sometimes years. Graffiti you see in towns and communities typically takes little time and little skill to generate and contributes to the visual blight within cities. Some communities in the United States have found solutions that contribute visual improvement and also demonstrate that this work can take time. One example of this is The Philadelphia Department of Recreation Mural Arts Program (MAP). This public art program works in partnership with community residents, grassroots organizations, government agencies, educational institutions, corporations and philanthropies to design and create murals of enduring value while actively engaging youth in the process. Those who participate in these efforts come to a clearer understanding of just how much time it takes to create the art that people see.

29

Purchasing Flower Power!

Grade Level
5-6

Classroom Time
One or two 40-min. periods

Materials/Tools
for 24-30 students

- Coffee filters
- Crayola® Classic Washable Markers
- Crayola Colored Pencil Classpack®
- Crayola Fabric Crayons
- Crayola Glitter Glue
- Crayola Model Magic® Value Pack (optional)
- Green floral tape
- Hole punch
- Iron (for adult use only)
- Newsprint
- Oaktag

Tips
Apply pressure when coloring coffee filters to achieve best color results.

Place newsprint under drawing paper for better control during coloring.

Resources
Longwood Gardens website: *www.longwoodgardens.org*

Rocket Minds™: Spin, Spend, and Earn (ages 8+); *Think-ama-Jink Checkers* (ages 6+)

Vase of Flowers, Jan Davidsz de Heem reproduction, p. 46

Visual Arts Standard 5
Mathematics Standards
Number and Operations
Problem Solving

Objective

Children create flowers and assign them values, then compute and show place value with decimals as they estimate and calculate the cost of flowers and bouquets.

Teacher Preparation

Classroom Teacher: With student assistance, create simple paper $5, $10, and $20 bills.

Art Teacher: Display pictures of flower arrangements that contain more than 3 flowers. Display other artifacts that illustrate radial design.

Discussion Starters

Classroom Teacher: Sometimes florists sell flowers by the stem. Typically when you send flowers to someone you send a bouquet. Is it less expensive to buy individual stems of flowers or do you think it is a better value to buy a bouquet of flowers? Where could you go to find out? Who is willing to do some research on this? Let's think about and calculate the cost of making a bouquet while you try to stay within a budget. I'll give each of you play money to spend.

Art Teacher: In class you learned about the cost of buying flowers by the stem versus buying a bouquet. Today we are going to make several single-stem flowers that demonstrate radial design. Then you will price your flower stems individually. With those flowers, you will put together beautiful bouquets—but the cost of the entire bouquet must not exceed your assigned budget! Create some unusual blossoms so you can pretend to purchase "flowers with power."

Process

Create flower blossoms

1. Study samples of radial designs.
2. Cover art surface with newsprint or newspaper. Press a coffee filter flat on the surface. Color radial designs on one side of the filter with fabric crayons.
3. Follow the instructions and cautions on the Fabric Crayon packaging. Cover filter with clean paper on a surface suitable for ironing. Ask an adult to iron the filter with a hot iron in a well-ventilated area. Press design with slow steady pressure for 1 to 2 minutes. Unfold filter while crayon is warm.
4. To add more design interest, fold coffee filter several times. Press washable colored marker nib against the folded filter and hold in position so filter absorbs dye. Unfold filter to reveal radial designs made with markers.
5. Apply a damp paper towel to diffuse dyes for added color effects. Air-dry filter completely.
6. Decorate blossom center and edges with glitter glue.
7. Repeat to make multiple blossoms.

Create the stem and price tag

1. Gather finished blossom into a cone shape. Squeeze pointed end against the top of a colored pencil barrel.
2. Wrap about 6 to 8 inches of floral tape around the gathered filter and top of the pencil to attach blossom to pencil.
3. Cut 1 x 2-inch rectangles of oak tag to create price tags. Punch a hole in one end of tag and insert ribbon or yarn. Create a decorative border on both sides of price tag. Decide the price of flower stem and write price on tag using decimal points on one side and ¢ signs on the other. Tie price tag to flower stem. Repeat for all blossoms.
4. Calculate the cost of buying several flowers while staying within the predetermined budget (play money provided by teacher).

Artwork by students from PS 132K, Brooklyn, NY.
Teacher: Charlotte Ka

Assessment

Children summarize what they learned in each step of this process. Ask students to select from stems created by classmates to calculate how many flowers they can purchase while staying within budget. Classmates meet in small groups to verify that they created at least one bouquet that stayed within their budgets.

Background Information

Most flowers arrive at your local flower shop from great distances. Florists get their stock from wholesalers, who obtain flowers and plants from huge international auctions.

The largest flower auction in the world is in Aalsmeer, Holland. Imagine an auction building that covers 160 acres, with complex computerized moving and tracking systems for their fragile wares. About 14 million flowers are auctioned every day in Aalsmeer—that's 3 billion flowers a year! Most of these flowers are shipped to other countries, including the United States.

Your favorite, fragrant flower in a Mother's Day bouquet or wedding arrangement may have been grown in Bulgaria, auctioned in Holland, flown by jet across the ocean, and then trucked to your hometown.

Personal Illusions— Raising Your Banner High

Grade Level
5-6

Classroom Time
Two to three 40-min. periods

Materials/Tools
for 24-30 students
- 30 18" x 24" pieces of fabric (cut up clean white bed sheets)
- 30 36" pieces of yarn or ribbon
- 30 sheets 12" x 18" white drawing paper
- Crayola® Fabric Crayons
- Crayola Fabric Markers
- Crayola Glitter Glue
- Crayola School Glue
- Iron (for adult use only) (optional)
- Newsprint
- White paper
- Very fine grade sandpaper sheets (optional)

Tip
Place fabric on newsprint or on a very fine grade of sandpaper to help keep it from gathering and slipping while drawing.

Resources
Trompe l'Oeil paintings on the National Gallery website: *www.nga.gov* (search "Harnet")

Images of Deception: The Art of Trompe l'Oeil
by Celestine Dars

Rocket Minds™: Think-ama-Jink Checkers (age 6+)

Japanese Textile Banners reproductions, pp. 36-37

Visual Arts Standard 6
Mathematics Standards
   Algebra
   Reasoning and Proof

Objective

Children use line, shape, color, and texture to create a personal standard/banner that illustrates an algebraic problem. Students analyze how lines are used to create shapes, and how shapes are used to create the illusion of 3-D forms, e.g., $(A + B) + (A + B) = C$

Teacher Preparation

Classroom Teacher: Make a bulletin board that shows the following: $(A + B) + (A + B) = C$ (horizontal line + vertical line) + (horizontal line + vertical line) = square

Art Teacher: Create a poster with student help that illustrates line drawings of the following 3-D forms: cone, cube, cylinder, pyramid, egg form, sphere, and rectangular prism. Write names of objects on separate pieces of paper and tack to board. Measure and cut one clean cotton sheet of fabric into 18" x 24" pieces for each child in class.

Discussion Starters

Classroom Teacher: Who can explain what kind of lines you need to make a square? A cylinder? A cone? When we combine lines, we create shapes. Following this same logic, when we combine shapes together we can create the illusion of 3-D forms on a flat surface.

Art Teacher: In class you talked about combining lines to make shapes and combining shapes to create the illusion of 3-D form. By combining these illusions, you can create identifiable objects such as figures, animals, and plants. Let's experiment with making some illusions of form to create a personal banner. The banner will reflect which lines, shapes, colors, textures, and 3-D illusions appeal to you.

Process

1. Place fabric on newsprint or very fine grade sandpaper sheets. Create two large rectangles, one above the other, with a 3-inch space separating the shapes and a 1 1/2-inch border above the top rectangle.
2. Think about combinations of lines that create shapes. Draw several shapes in the top rectangle using fabric crayons.
3. Reflect on your shapes, and then think about combinations of shapes that create the illusion of 3-D forms. Draw these in the bottom rectangle using fabric markers.
4. Optional step: Follow the instructions and cautions on the Fabric Crayon packaging. Sandwich the fabric between two sheets of newsprint. Ask an adult to iron the fabric to set the color. Set iron on synthetic. Iron only in a well-ventilated area. Press design with slow steady pressure for 1 to 2 minutes. Lift iron to move it. Hold papers in place to prevent blurring. Remove paper carefully. Consider enriching the design by drawing directly with a fabric crayon while the fabric is still warm, but not hot.
5. Roll the drawing paper and glue together to form a cylinder.
6. Apply glue to a 1-inch top border of the fabric. Place the paper cylinder onto the glued border and roll. Air dry thoroughly.
7. Thread 3-foot long ribbon or yarn through the cylinder and tie closed to hang.

Assessment

Have children summarize their learning. Ask children to list the lines they needed to create shapes, the shapes they needed to create forms, and the forms they needed to create identifiable objects. Students exchange papers and banners and check to see if their formulas match.

Artwork by students from CS 103, Bronx, NY.
Teacher: Neila Steiner

Quote

It is the rare child that understands the close relationship between math and art. I've often watched children try to draw something familiar, look at their art and say, "I don't like it, that's not what it looks like," and stop working or ask for another paper. It is often very frustrating trying to translate a three-dimensional world onto a two-dimensional surface. Most children need to be shown how to add a third dimension to a two-dimensional surface. Once they develop the understanding of how to create the illusion, primarily through math concepts, their art takes off along with the satisfaction of making things look "real".
—Neila Steiner, CS102, Project ARTS Coordinator, Bronx, NY

Background Information

Some artists are so skillful at creating illusions that they fool the viewer into thinking they see three-dimensional objects in real space. This is a method of painting called "Trompe l'Oeil," which means "fool the eye."

Because a painting is on a flat (two-dimensional) surface, it takes a lot of observation, planning, and even mathematical skill to create these illusions. Throughout history, artists have used various devices to help them duplicate the look of three-dimensional objects, or to create the illusion that one object was close and another very far away.

In fact, the invention of photography owes much to a device used by artists for centuries, called a "camera obscura," which enabled them to project an image in a darkened room through a tiny hole in one wall.

Above: Quilt, circa 1965, by Mary L. Bennett of Gee's Bend, Alabama. Cotton and cotton/polyester blend. 77" x 82" Reproduced by permission of Tinwood Ventures.

Right: Quilt, circa 1955, by Sue Willie Seltzer of Gee's Bend, Alabama. Cotton and synthetic blends. 80" x 76" inches. Reproduced by permission of Tinwood Ventures.

Above: *Woman* by Joan Miró, Gift of George L. Erion, Image © 2003 Board of Trustees, National Gallery of Art, Washington, D.C. 1976, oil on canvas, 60" x 72"; framed 60 5/8" x 73 1/2"

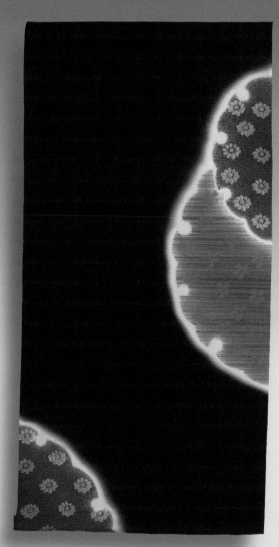

Left: Japanese Textile Banner, 2001 by unknown artisan. Paint on silk brocade. 15" x 39 ¼". Kyoto, Japan. Private Collection.

Above: Japanese Textile Banner, 2001 by unknown artisan. Paint on silk brocade. 15" x 25 ½". Kyoto, Japan, 2001. Private Collection.

Top Left: Japanese Textile Banner, 2001 by unknown artisan. Paint on dyed silk. 15" x 31". Kyoto, Japan. Private Collection.

Bottom Left: Detail of Japanese Textile Banner, 2001

Right: Japanese Textile Banner, 2001 by unknown artisan. Paint on dyed silk. 15" x 68". Kyoto, Japan. Private Collection.

See lesson on page 32: "Personal Illusions – Raising Your Banner High"

Bottom: "1905" Hanging Picture Frame Beaded Whimsy, circa early 1900's. High relief glass beading on shocking pink cotton field. 10" x 6¼". Collection of Dr. Thomas Schantz.

Right Top: "Fox Box" with Lid and Handles Beaded Whimsy, circa early 1900's. Glass beading on electric pink cotton field, 7" x 5½" x 8" including loops. Collection of Dr. Thomas Schantz.

Right Bottom: Detail of "Fox Box"

Above: Tri-lobe Heart Hanging Pincushion Whimsy, circa early 1900's. Glass beading on pink field. 8" x 8 ¼" x 3". Collection of Dr. Thomas Schantz.

Right: "From Niagara Falls" Hanging Shoe Pincushion Whimsy, circa early 1900's. Glass beading on purple velvet field. 7 ½" x 6 ¼" x 2 ¼". Collection of Dr. Thomas Schantz.

See lesson on page 20: "Whimsical Charting and Checking"

Left: "Andy Gump" Toy, circa 1930's. Cast iron. 7 ¼" x 3 ¾" x 6". Collection of Rudy Clark.

Below: Daytona Silver Bullet Speedster Toy, circa 1921-22. Paint on fabricated tin. 25 ¾" x 5 ¾" x 4". Collection of Rudy Clark.

Above (Left to Right): Auburn Speedster. circa 1938. Fabricated colored rubber. 11" x 3¾" x 2½"; Indianapolis Race Car, circa 1947. Painted fabricated tin and rubber. 18" x 7¾" x 6½"; Indianapolis Race Car, circa 1912-15. Painted fabricated tin. 11¾" x 4½" x 4½". All, collection of Rudy Clark.

Bottom: Steam Powered Shovel Toy, circa 1931. Fabricated tin and cotton cord. 20" x 7" x 14", Collection of Rudy Clark.

See lesson on page 24: "Toying Around With Geometry"

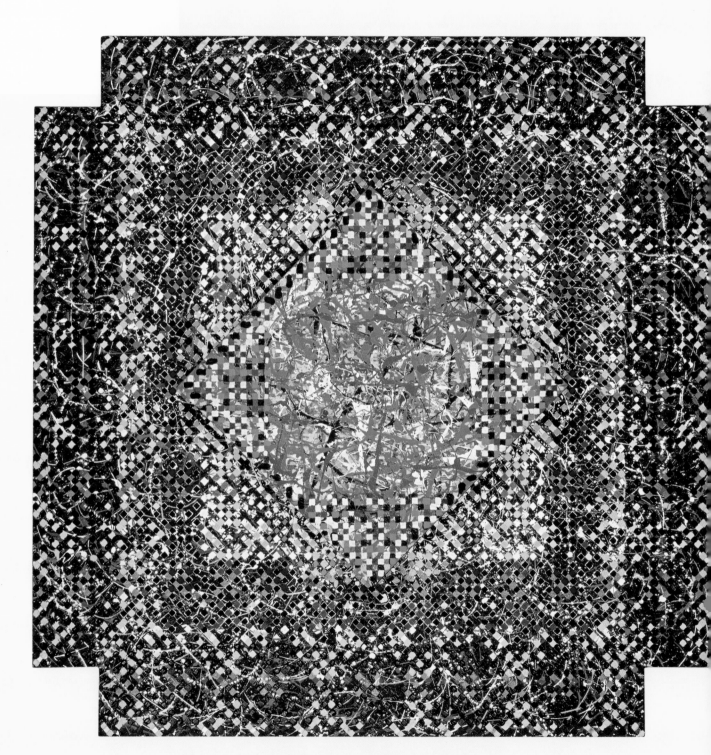

Above: *Beside the Still Waters*, 1984-2003, by Kendall Shaw. Acrylic and mirrors on canvas. 60" x 60". Collection of the artist.

Above: *Sun Ship*, 1982, by Kendall Shaw. Acrylic and mirrors on canvas.
4 panels, total 101" X 101". Collection of the artist.

See lesson on page 26: "Measure Twice, Create Once"

Above: *Lilium canadense L* (Meadow Lily). Glass with mixed media. Ware Collection of Blaschka Glass Models of Plants. Circa 1886. By Leopold and Rudolph Blaschka. Harvard Museum of Natural History, Cambridge, MA. Copyright President and Fellows of Harvard College. Photograph by Hillel Burger.

Left: *Iris versicolor L – Iris* (Fleur-de-lis). Glass with mixed media. Ware Collection of Blaschka Glass Models of Plants. Circa 1886. By Leopold and Rudolph Blaschka. Harvard Museum of Natural History, Cambridge, MA. Copyright President and Fellows of Harvard College. Photograph by Hillel Burger.

Bottom: Detail of *Iris versicolor L – Iris*

Above: *Nymphaea odorata ait* (Fragrant Water Lily). Glass
with mixed media. Ware Collection of Blaschka Glass Models
of Plants. Circa 1886. By Leopold and Rudolph Blaschka. Harvard
Museum of Natural History, Cambridge, MA. Copyright President and
Fellows of Harvard College. Photograph by
Hillel Burger.

See lesson on page 30: "Purchasing Flower Power"

Above: *Vase of Flowers* by Jan Davidsz de Heem. Andrew W. Mellon Fund.
Image ©2003 Board of Trustees, National Gallery of Art, Washington, D.C.
c.1660, oil on canvas, 27 ⅜" x 22 ¼"; framed 35 ½" x 30" x ⅝"

Above: Floral Motif Textile from Kashmir, India (artisan unknown). Contemporary, date unknown. Private Collection.

See lesson on page 10: "Counting on a Spectacular Garden"

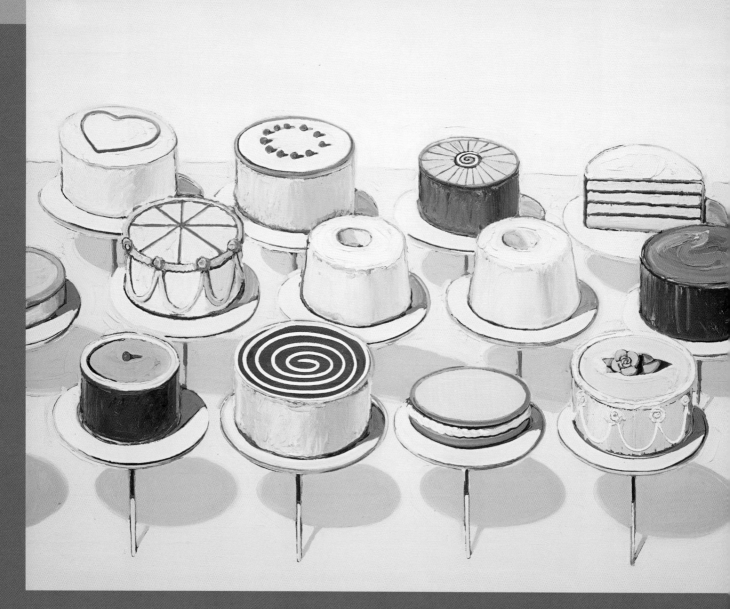

Above: *Cakes* by Wayne Thiebaud, Gift in Honor of the 50th Anniversary of the National Gallery of Art from the Collectors Committee, the 50th Anniversary Gift Committee, and The Circle, with Additional Support from the Abrams Family in Memory of Harry N. Abrams, Image © 2003 Board of Trustees, National Gallery of Art, Washington, D.C. 1963, oil on canvas, 60″ x 72″; framed 60 5/8″ x 73″ x 1/2″